There once was a young lad, who was of a royal priesthood in his homeland in Africa, who was brought as a slave in shackles and chains to America. He is only known as Prince. From him came a son named David. From him came a son named John Andy. From him came a son named George. And from these forefathers came a daughter named Mable Ann. And the rest is history.

Sharecropper

by Mable Ann Hemphill

Warren Publishing, Inc.

Copyright © 2015
Mable Ann Hemphill

All rights reserved. No part of this publication may be reproduced, stored in a retrieval system, or transmitted in any form or any other means electronic, mechanical, photocopying, recording or otherwise, without the prior written permission of the publisher.

Published by Warren Publishing, Inc.
Charlotte, NC
www.warrenpublishing.net

ISBN: 978-1-943258-09-3

Library of Congress Control Number: 2015949742

Published by Warren Publishing, Inc.
www.warrenpublishing.net

Contents

Acknowledgments i

Introduction 1

Inauguration Day 6

Tin Roof 11

Maid in America 14

Pete 16

Communion Sunday 18

The Tea Set 22

Out in Left Field 24

Letters to My Teachers... Mrs. Sanders 27

Kool-Aid and Bible School 29

Fried Pies 31

Strawberry Story 33

Letters to My Teachers...Mrs. Smith 43

False Teeth and the Singing Convention 46

Didn't I Tell Y'all? 48

Raleigh Man 51

Letters to My Teachers...Mr. Brown 54

Let the Lord Do His Work 57

Angel with the Strange Arms 59

Soda Water 62

Medicinal Purposes 67

Letters to My Teachers...Mrs. Norman 73

A Negro Killing in a Southern Town 76

His Plan 79

About the Author 84

ACKNOWLEDGEMENTS

All praises, honors and credit to the Most High God.

Many thanks to my parents, George Bigger and Deloris Bigger, now Mrs. Warren B. Stewart. To my children, Jarvis Hemphill and Leslie, Cherrish Slade, and Darrow. To my guardian angel, Mr. Pink Johnson, for believing in my endeavors. To my love and my confidant, Mr. James T. Hamer, for your unconditional love and 'wit' to make me laugh. And to my best friend of sixty plus years, Sally. Thank you for being you.

To great-great-grandfather Prince, a slave; great-grandparents David, born in 1863, free but not free, and Rosalind Bigger; grandparents John Andy, born in 1889, and Mary Gwinn Bigger.

To four teachers, among other educators, who loved their profession and made a difference in the lives of every child they taught. They made it their one goal to let every child know how much they were loved and respected, regardless of their home life. Taking that child under their own wing, sometimes taking money from their own pockets or time from their own family, they made sure she was given the tools she needed to succeed in life. Mrs. Sanders, my 2nd grade teacher; Mrs. Matrue Smith, my 3rd grade teacher; Mr. Wilbur Lewis Brown, my 8th grade teacher; Mrs. Barbara Norman, my Biology teacher. You saw in me what I could not see in myself.

Mr. Pink Johnson (deceased before the book got published) for your computer skills.

INTRODUCTION

As the child (I was raised as their child, not their grandchild) of a gentle giant of a sharecropper, born in 1889, who had lived through the times of not being allowed to walk with his head held high as a young boy, having to cross to the other side of the street if a white woman was coming his way or else he could have been beaten or lynched, a so called "boy" who was sent as a man to fight for the country he loved not feeling that it loved him, returning an Army veteran "boy" to the fields of the south to the only profession he knew which allowed him to keep his family alive.

He was a sharecropper who came from a long line of sharecroppers. His father had been killed on his way home, returning to the 'shanty' of the home he loved. He was born in 1863. On the night he was killed, he had gone to put the horses up for the night after a long hard day (daytime started before 5am and ended after sundown) of plowing the fields while only stopping to get a cool drink of water from a dried gourd made into a dipper. His father was a slave known only to him as "Prince".

He was an army veteran sharecropper man among men who lived and married a woman among women known to some as Miss Mae or Mae Bigger but called by me and my brothers as Mommae, who came from Hickory Grove, South Carolina. She was illiterate somewhat (you had to discern what her writing was and it took you awhile to figure out what she was saying in the message) but she got her point across. An Army sharecropper wife and a "colored woman" whose only skill was that of being a maid to white families and hoeing and picking cotton. She never knew the impact that working as a maid would make on a country that was in itself going through "years" of transition.

She was uneducated because she was not given the opportunity of 'schooling' but she possessed a 'mother's wit'.

This book is dedicated to the memory of the both of them and to all the sharecroppers, whether black, very poor whites, American Indians, folks of all ethnicities. Whether they came to this land on the boats from Africa "tight pack" or hidden from the world searching for a better life for themselves and generations after them.

All of them worked tirelessly day in and day out to make this country great. Because of them, we are now living in the "greatest" country in the world. They touched the lives of others and perpetuated what it means when we hear those words "My country tis' of thee, sweet land of liberty, of the I sing."

It is dedicated: To all of those whose lives and professions built the "White House" but were never allowed to walk proudly as a citizen of this great country of ours.

……To those, who during previous years, worked the farms of others as sharecroppers but never "owned the farm" or reaped the "real harvest" that they worked for.

…To the single mothers of earlier years, who lived in the south, who had no help from the fathers of their children, but worked in the fields and in the homes of others, having to disregard their own children and leave them with "Big Momma" or the eldest child, while working the fields, cleaning the houses, cooking the meals of others, then coming home tired, worn out from working all day for $2 dollars a day (if anything) or room and board for the family, then taking what she could and sometimes taking dried beans, flour and water and making a meal of beans and dumplings.

... To the young widowed "colored" mothers of the south who in after 1863 and early 1900's who husbands were share croppers but died leaving her behind to fend for herself and her children with no help, no skills and no known resources to keep her family alive so she had to accept the advances of the owner of the land who was kind enough to keep her and the children with "enough" to live off of sometimes more when a light skinned or almost white child accidently showed up in her household.

...To all of the sharecroppers who toiled tirelessly day and night with calloused hands and feet, never knowing what tomorrow would bring but working anyway for a better tomorrow, I take this time to say "Thank You" for working, never complaining, never being recognized for all that you did for this country and its citizens and to make this country of which I love, the greatest country in the world, THE UNITED STATES OF AMERICA.

...But most of all I take this time to remember, reflect upon, and never forget but always remember The Honorable John Andy and Mary Gwinn Bigger, a sickly Army Veteran and an illiterate maid. Sharecroppers who lived in the rural south who did the best they could, with what little they had, to raise this skinny legged, now African American then "colored girl" to be the woman I am today.

TO PAWPAW AND MOMMAE, from your baby girl, THIS ONE'S FOR YOU!!!!!

Inauguration Day

The day was January 20th, 2009. As I got ready, like so many others, to go to Washington DC and bear witness to the inauguration of our first African American president of these United States, I took a moment to reflect.

If they had been alive, PawPaw and Mommae and my other ancestors would have loved to witness this. So would my ancestor, Prince, who was royal in his homeland but brought to this country as a slave. So would Great-Grandpa David, who was run over and killed on his way home from a hard day's work. They never even thought this day would come. I began to wonder, did our president know what it took to get all of us to this day, and how many people had lost their very lives during the journey?

He had never even heard of the old Zion Hill School house, a one room shanty of a place where colored students in the late 1920's and 1930's got up to an eighth, but mostly only sixth grade education. But they were proud of it. They even had a school slogan: "It takes more than a local school to make Zion Hill tear it's record down."

What was our new president feeling?

He might have met Jackie Robinson, but he had never even heard about the Sally League in the South or the Stateline Sluggers, a Negro League of some of the best baseball players in America. My father was one of them, and their names will never be forgotten by their families.

Did he know that, years before, in the night, my grandparents helped organize a faithful few into the NAACP of our area in their three room shack on Ridge Road in Clover, South Carolina? I still have the tattered Bible holding their signatures to prove it.

Did he know how coloreds in the South had gone to the back lots to get food from so-called restaurants? And if your food got dropped on the ground as they were handing it to you through a small window, you didn't get any food at all, or your money back.

Did he even have a clue how people of color had, tired though they may be, plowed the fields, raising bloody calluses on their hands, walking behind a horse or two, day in and day out, with it being hot as two hells, only stopping to get a drink of water and a piece of bread?

Did he even stop to think about the sharecropper of color, whose day started before sun-up so he could pick two to three hundred pounds of cotton by the end of it? Then he would dump his sack into a sheet from the cotton gin, which was spread on the ground before being bundled up, weighed, and hoisted onto the shoulders of two more sharecroppers to carry away for counting. All so he could meet his quota by the end of the week and bring home maybe twenty dollars. And that was considered a lot of money back then.

I wondered, did he know about the maids of color like my grandmother? Who, even though worn out, with veins sticking out on their legs from being on their feet mostly all day every day, had toiled tirelessly, with rags on their heads and cotton stockings knotted around their legs as they worked, to feed "the future" who would go on to become great leaders.

Did he fathom the sheer magnitude of this day, and what events had taken place in order to get him and the

United States of America and the world here, to *this* moment in time?

That is when I pulled out the pictures and looked at my own life, and what it had taken to get me from being called n*****, to negro to colored, to now, African American.

I didn't know how to honor the real trailblazers who had gone on before. The real pioneers, who lay in the grave, but whose spirit was still alive and moving. I thought, *What could I do? I am one person sitting here.*

But PawPaw and Mommae were colored sharecroppers who, like so many others, had a dream. A dream of a better life for their children, grandchildren, and generations to come. A dream of better days to come for all people regardless of their race or their upbringing.

What could I do to honor them and to keep their dream within me and alive? I wanted our new president and the rest of the world to know just what it took. No one knew them or what they did to make this day possible.

That's when I decided, and said to myself, "They worked so hard for this day, I got to take them with me." So I got my coat and some safety pins and found a place on the coat for my pictures. I told PawPaw and Mommae that I would get something that no one else could get, and keep it for them in remembrance of this day: a pebble.

But I brought back more than just a pebble for PawPaw and Mommae that day. I brought back their memories. Their stories on the tongues Americans from all over our country and from all walks of life. And now, in this book, those stories will never be forgotten.

Tin Roof

By the time I was born, PawPaw and Mommae had been sharecroppers for years. For a while, there was no one but PawPaw, Mommae, and me under one roof because we had moved away from my parents and my brother. And I literally mean one roof; I can't remember any insulation. But we always had so much love for each other that I never knew or felt like we were poor. Plus, all the other colored sharecroppers who lived around us lived the same way, in what most people would consider shanties. But to us it was home.

I remember one day when Mommae was away working, either in the field or in some white lady's house, the sky started to look dark. We were living in the first three room shanty that I remember, and I say this with much pride because we were never homeless. Mommae had left me and PawPaw some breakfast and dinner on the table in the kitchen near the shelf with the tin water bucket and dipper.

PawPaw was real sick that day, and Mommae had to go to work so she left me to watch over him and hand him things when he needed. She trusted me because, even though I was a young child, she had trained me to be the helper of our small household.

I remember it like it was yesterday. PawPaw was in the kitchen part of the house trying to heat up the fish on the wood stove. It was a wood stove that had an oven and places on the top to set pots and pans. That meant you had to make a fire in the stove. It had a gauge on the front of the oven door to tell you the temperature so you would not let the fire get too hot. Mommae usually kept it going all Saturday, making us a lot of pies and cakes for Sunday.

Most sharecroppers cooked their Sunday vegetables on Saturday night and fried their chicken early on Sunday morning. Some sharecropper wives did no cooking on Sunday because we went to church almost all day, so they cooked on Saturday night.

Anyway, Mommae and my aunt had gone fishing and caught some the day before for us to eat, and PawPaw was heating it up when a big gust of wind went rushing by. Or at least, that is what I thought. I looked up and saw the sky!

That big ole' gust of wind had come through and snatched the tin roof so far back that the clouds were smiling at us. You remember how we used to get sardines in a can with the key on top and you'd insert the key and peel back the lid? Well that is what the wind did to that tin roof! I remember PawPaw getting me by one hand and our tin plate of fish and a few biscuits in the other, and we walked as fast as we could to the nearby neighbors house. Although, he couldn't walk too fast because he couldn't breathe too good and had been sick that morning.

Thank God that even though the wind was blowing something awful, it never rained. We couldn't stay at home that day, and Mommae was a proud Army and sharecropper's wife so we couldn't accept much charity, and we never got any welfare. But someone came and put the roof back on our humble little abode and we were happy again.

Maid in America

Long before Abraham Lincoln gave his address at Gettysburg, before George Washington Carver and his peanut, before our most gracious First Lady Obama was even a thought in her parents mind, there arose a woman of great substance and true grit known as the maid.

Having mostly no education, this resourceful pioneer worked long hours for little pay, no pay during slavery, leaving her own children with others so she could put food on her table.

Although there was no escaping the educational boundaries, she used her "mother's wit" to mold the lives of the families whom God himself had entrusted to her care.

She would measure ingredients to the nearest crumb without even dropping a spot of flour on the floor, or on her starched and ironed apron.

Her biscuits filled empty stomachs of future doctors who would heal the sicknesses of the United States of America and the world. Her pies would put smiles on the faces of great world leaders. Little did she know of the power she had in her hands as she spent her time cooking and cleaning, never complaining, even though she was thought of as simply a domestic worker.

Looking back into our country's history, my history, and your own family's history, take time to be thankful and salute the heroes who worked without knowing the full impact they would have.

This phenomenal caretaker and caregiver known as the maid helped to make and mold the greatest country in the world, the United States of America. And one of these remarkable women was my grandmother, Mary Gwinn Bigger.

PETE

For sharecroppers' children in the early 1920's, and for the next thirty to forty years, there was never much play time when the weather was good. The land owners made sure that a sharecropper kept his children working. The sons of the sharecroppers were always plowing the field while the landowner's kids went to school.

But with my grandparents, our life was a bit different, plus I was very young when we moved away from my parents. It seems that PawPaw and Mommae always had some type of animal for me to pet or to play with. I remember PawPaw once got me a pet calf. Or so I thought. I called him Pete, and he was such a cute little thing! I would go to the pasture a few feet away from our house all during the day and talk with him. I got to feed him and love on him , too.

Well, Pete keep getting larger and larger in everyone's eyes, but to me he was still my pet calf. Then one day Pete went missing. A few weeks later, on a Sunday, the preacher and his wife came to our humble abode for dinner and Mommae had cooked one of her bestest meals ever. We had two meats that day. I thought we were rich!

The following Monday, I made it my small business to look for Pete. I couldn't go but so far, but I looked high and low for my dear pet. Finally, PawPaw said, "Mae, if you don't tell that chap where that animal is, I will."

That was when my world collapsed, for Pete had been our Sunday dinner.

Communion Sunday

All of us sharecropper kids loved Communion Sunday, which happened on the first Sunday of every month.

During this service, the elder men always sat on the front pew, and the ladies sat in the pews off to the side. The ladies would be all dressed in white, with white hats on their heads. It was the custom for ladies, if they were stewardesses or deaconesses, to cover their heads in church, especially on the first Sunday.

What we children loved about Communion Sunday was getting something to eat and drink. It was like a small picnic. We loved drinking grape juice from the tiny cups and eating pieces of cracker. Not to mention there would always be some juice and crackers leftover from the service.

So, immediately afterward, all of the kids would go around to the back to the kitchen door, and the nice ladies who prepared communion would give us the extra food.

I think they saved this on purpose because they knew we were coming.

We had Heaven on earth. Although, it was curious that the crackers had no salt on them like the saltine cracker we ate at home. But we didn't care. We just continued to enjoy our after church communion lunch, and went home with our tummies full.

Thank you, ladies of Liberty Hill AME Zion Church in Clover, South Carolina, for making all of us kids happy.

Communion Sunday

All us sharecropper kids loved Communion Sunday, which happened on the first Sunday of every month.

During this service, the elder men always sat on the front pew, and the ladies sat in the pews off to the side. The ladies would be all dressed in white, with white hats on their heads. It was the custom for ladies, if they were stewardesses or deaconesses, to cover their heads in church, especially on the first Sunday.

What we children loved about Communion Sunday was getting something to eat and drink. It was like a small picnic. We loved drinking grape juice from the tiny cups and eating pieces of cracker. Not to mention there would always be some juice and crackers leftover from the service.

So, immediately afterward, all of the kids would go around to the back to the kitchen door, and the nice ladies who prepared communion would give us the extra food.

I think they saved this on purpose because they knew we were coming.

We had Heaven on earth. Although, it was curious that the crackers had no salt on them like the saltine cracker we ate at home. But we didn't care. We just continued to enjoy our after church communion lunch, and went home with our tummies full.

Thank you, ladies of Liberty Hill AME Zion Church in Clover, South Carolina, for making all of us kids happy.

The Tea Set

Sally and I have been best friends for over 60 years or it will be by the time this book goes to print. We still have wonderful times.

One of the best times of our lives was the time Sally's mom bought her a tea set.

That particular day was in the summertime in Clover, South Carolina on the Ridge Road where a lot of sharecropper families lived and raised their families. We were probably 5 or 6 years old at the time and Sally's mother was cooking dinner. It was around noon because the people who worked the field would come home for dinner if they were close by.

Her mom had made a delicious dinner for her husband, Sally's father and my Godfather, Roosevelt. He had been working in the field, picking either corn or cotton, I can't remember which.

She had a small table for us to eat from, set up in the front yard where she could keep an eye on us. She surprised us that day with a pretty tea set for two. She not only surprised us with the tea set, but with food that went along with it.

We had pinto beans and cabbage and hot biscuits. But she had made the biscuits especially for our small hands. Plus she had made some nice sweet tea for our little tea cups. We were so excited!! We thought that we were rich and lived somewhere grand, like in a big castle.

We may not have been rich with money or lived in a castle, but we were rich with love in our hearts for Sally's mom and appreciation of the tasty food in our tummies. Something tells me that we went inside and took a nap. Here I am in my 60's and I still remember those good times growing up as the granddaughter of a sharecropper in rural Clover, South Carolina. Dedicated to Roosevelt and Minnie Kendrick and their unconditional love for me Miss Mable Ann.

Out in Left Field

Young black men, called colored boys many years ago, loved to play baseball as much as the white boys.

If they were really good, they played in the Sally League, which was part of the National Negro Baseball League. You may have heard of some of its players, one of whom was Jackie Robinson.

It just so happens that one of these sharecropper baseball players was my father. George Washington Bigger came into this world in Clover, South Carolina. Our best records say he was born on June 28th, 1928.

His real mother was named Mable, after whom I am respectfully named, but she died of tuberculosis when he was nine years old. They lived in the little house by the Big Oak Tree off highway 55, or 557, in Clover, South Carolina. His father married Mary Gwinn, and she and PawPaw raised my father.

We are absolutely sure of my father's birth date because for a long time in the rural South, when a colored boy grew old enough to enter the military, the white landowner on whose farm the boy lived and worked the fields could, and would sometimes, change his birth date to keep him on the farm. This happened to my father, which could either be a good thing or a bad thing, depending on how you looked at it.

Anyway, my father played with the renowned Stateline Sluggers. This team was known for winning. They had some of the best players this side of the Mason/Dixon line. My father played left field. Folks who knew him said he could run fast with his skinny, bow legs, and catch a ball no matter how high the sun was, or how bright it was shinning in his eyes. My father had big eyes.

He also went to Zion Hill School. That is how I found out about the school slogan: "It takes more than a local school to make Zion Hill tear its record down."

Those were the days when the players who traveled could not even think about going into a white restaurant to eat, or ever go inside a public place to use a restroom or get a drink of water.

But these players will never be forgotten in our hearts. They are the true pioneers of national baseball history, and they made the best of a sometimes bad situation.

So, for a left fielder known as Chicken George, who played with the Stateline Sluggers in Clover, South Carolina, may you rest in much deserved peace from your labor. The bar was set high during segregation and the early 1900's in the history of Southern baseball.

I respectfully dedicate this segment to the memory of the Stateline Sluggers.

Letters to My Teachers from the Sharecropper's Desk

Second Grade Classroom

Roosevelt School

Dear Mrs. Sanders,

Thank you for being so kind.

You were always so very pretty, with such a pretty smile. But what I will always remember about you is that you gave each child a hug in the morning before class. It made our day.

Like all the other teachers at Roosevelt School, you always made sure we began each day with the Pledge of Allegiance.

You made sure that everyone had a writing tablet, and one of those big pencils with big erasers on them. And you always kept extra for the poorer children.

Even when some of the boys who couldn't read well fell asleep at their desks because they had to work most of the time on the farm where their family were sharecroppers, you never embarrassed them or belittled them because you knew their struggles.

For this, and for giving so much to so many, I most humbly thank you.

   Sincerely,
   Miss Mable Ann

Kool-Aid and Bible School

One of my fondest memories growing up as a sharecropper was attending Bible school in the summer. It seemed as if every kid wanted to go to Bible School. Well, you might as well like it because you had to go anyway; elderly sharecropper grandparents and parents never let you skip going to Bible School.

All the kids, both big and little, would walk from a long way up the road to Mt. Harmony Church to go to Bible School. Mt. Harmony Cemetery is the place where some of my ancestors are buried, and it was a hundred years old back then, so it must be going on two hundred years old, now.

School was taught by this real nice Christian lady. All the kids loved her. She was so smart. The kids who couldn't read real good were always given help with reading by this nice lady. She taught us a song called "Nummy." I never knew why we sang it or what it was about, but it was fun. She taught us to always sing songs and to love one another.

But the most important thing to us kids was lunch. We always had a glass of grape Kool-Aid and half of a potted meat sandwich cut in a triangle. It was delicious!

I never knew how she could take a couple packs of Kool-Aid and make so many gallons of that tasty grape drink for so many kids. And trust me, it would be a lot of kids, both big and little. Some were teenagers, and no one acted up or disrespected her or any of the grown-ups.

Some of the kids were quite poor, so they didn't wear shoes in summer. No one really noticed anyway because we grew up not knowing who was poor. We all just lived the life of a sharecropping family.

Fried Pies

One of my cherished memories about growing up in the South is Sunday dinners. And other than fried chicken done Southern style, with some green beans and some of the best potato salad this side of the Mason/Dixon line, there is nothing better than "fried pies."

Southern mothers would get fruit, like apples, peaches, or pears, and peel and slice them. Then they'd put them on a covered piece of cardboard and lay them in the hot summer sun to dry. They would then store the fruit to be used at any given time, but mostly on Sunday, to make fried pies.

Fried pies back then were made with homemade biscuit dough rolled out on the table with a homemade roller and some flour. The fruit would have been cooked and seasoned with cinnamon, nutmeg, mace or allspice, sugar, and country butter. Then the fruit was spooned onto the pieces of dough, which were folded over and put into a hot cast iron frying pan full of grease. When the dough was golden brown, the pie was taken out, put on a plate, dusted with a little sugar, and served.

Kids thought they were in sweet Heaven when they ate those fried pies. My mouth still waters and a smile still comes to my face when I think about those days.

The Strawberry Story

"It takes a village..." We have heard this phrase so often. Well, I sincerely believe it holds true for sharecroppers, both abroad and most definitely here in these United States.

I cannot remember if this story is before PawPaw or after PawPaw, but here goes.

It was hot as all get out and we were all over to my aunt's house. They had a whole lot of kids, both big and little. There were six of them, eight of my other cousins, five kids from up the road who were equally as poor as we were, and the three of us. Now mind you, this was a way of life in the rural South among colored sharecroppers in the 1950's and before.

We were all outside, as was common, but on this day we had been in the other field looking for rabbit's tobacco and maypops. The oldest girl and her sister were inside cooking, and there were at least four adults working in the field.

Well, dinner time came and we were all hungry. In the sharecropper's home, no one ever was allowed to leave hungry, so they always shared whatever amount they had with others. But as always, before we ate, we washed our hands, bowed our heads, gave thanks, and blessed the food.

Now I know we had beans seasoned with meat or meat rinderins.' And we most definitely had good hot biscuits. But the one thing I will always remember was the dessert.

For some reason, on this day, we had something sweet. Most of the time, the children picked fruit that was canned and put up for winter. But on this day somebody had picked a "child's handful" of fresh strawberries and given them to the oldest girl. She always had a plan, and a knack for feeding a lot of people with a little bit of food. Little becomes much in the hands of a master.

Anyway, we were all called in to get something to eat. There were tin plates, glass jars, and tin cans to eat and drink from. We ate like kings! Then came dessert. We were all big-eyed.

To this day, I still don't know how she did it, but she had taken that child's handful of strawberries and, being the daughter of a sharecropper, cooked the biggest pie I have ever seen in my life. I never knew where she got the pan, but it was huge. Not to mention the strawberries. There couldn't have been more than twelve, fifteen at the most. And these were wild strawberries, not nursery strawberries, so they were small and real sweet.

Now, if you have done the math, there were a lot of hungry persons to feed, counting the kids and the adults, who had worked out in some field. How in the world she took twelve to fifteen tiny strawberries and fed so many is still a mystery. And we all got a good portion of dessert. Maybe some got only crust, top and bottom, and some good, real sweet, strawberry juice. But because of the gracious grace of an Almighty God and a master chef called Annie, I, Mable Ann, got a strawberry in mine. So we all went home with our bellies full and smiles on our faces.

Mable Ann Hemphill

My Grandparents' Marriage Certificate from 1937.
John Andy Bigger and Mary Gwinn Bigger.

Grandfather's sister, Aunt Cora.

Bottom Left: Mary Gwinn Bigger (my loving grandmother) teaching me to walk.

Bottom Right: My brother Mike Bigger (little boy in coat).

MABLE ANN HEMPHILL

PawPaw John Andy Bigger with my best friend Mrs. Sally Kendrick Graham, my brother Andy laying on PawPaw, me, Miss Mable and a cute little child (I forgot who).

Me, Miss Mable, sitting near a car in 1959 at Liberty Hill AME Zion Church.

Aunt Bill, my Uncle Henry's wife. She loved making me 'hot' Tang.

MABLE ANN HEMPHILL

Aunt Lena,
my father's sister.

Below: My Beautiful
Mother Mrs. Warren B.
Stewart.

My Grandmother, Mary Gwinn Bigger, with her grandchildren.

Mommae with my daughter Cherrish.

Above: Me in Washington. D.C. on President Barak Obama's first Inauguration.

Left: The Pebble.

Letters to My Teachers from the Sharecropper's Desk

Third Grade Classroom
Roosevelt School

Dear Mrs. Matrue Smith,

Thank you for your belief in thinking skills.

You were big on lesson planning. Every morning, we always knew what we were going to do for the day, since you always had our lessons planned out. But even though you taught us to plan, you also taught us to think. And you taught me and others to think outside of our surroundings.

I remember one time in particular, we had just come back to school after summer vacation. We were poor kids, so summer vacation meant not going to school, but also not going anywhere else.

When we sat down to our desks, you asked each child to write about something they had done while they were out of school. Nothing had changed in my small life, so I had nothing to write about. But since you had taught me to think outside of my surroundings, I wrote a poem. It was called "May is Fifth in Line." I was so proud! When my time came to read about my summer, I read my poem. You smiled, and took me by the hand, saying, "Mable, come with me."

You took me outside the classroom and asked, "Did you write that all by yourself?"

"Yes, m'am." I said.

Then we went back in the classroom and resumed the readings. You said you were so proud of everyone in the class, you told me to go home and tell my family to keep a look out for my name in the newspaper.

The only newspaper we read back then was the *Evening Herald*. PawPaw always read it. One day, much to my family's and our neighbors' amazement, there was my poem in the *Evening Herald!* My grandparents were so proud. Mommae couldn't read real well, so I read it to her. Even the white lady Mommae worked for was proud of me and told me to keep up the good work.

But it was because you taught me and other sharecropper kids to think outside of our surroundings that I had the courage, not only to write a poem back then, but to write a book and have it published now.

For still being the great teacher you are, even though you are no longer with me, I most humbly thank you.

    Sincerely,
    Miss Mable Ann

False Teeth and the Singing Convention

Some of the funniest memories in my life are from the days when PawPaw and Mommae and I would go to other churches for what was called a Singing Convention.

I was raised by many of my elders, as were most other sharecropper kids in those days. A lot of children were raised by grandparents back then because, sometimes, everyone lived in one house or on one landowners property.

Anyway, were going to the church for a singing, and this time there was preaching as well. A lot of other kids were there, too, but the old people knew not to let us all sit together. There would always be one kid in the group who was naughty, but it was never me or any of my cousins because my folk didn't stand for any shenanigans.

Well, this particular Sunday, they let us kids sit in the pews on the side because it was afternoon and they knew we were all going to fall asleep. Now mind you, this was in the days before air-conditioning. The church had fans in the windows to pull the heat out as much as possible, and then they gave out individual fans to all the older people.

I was just settling in for my afternoon nap, when I got a nudge from another kid to wake up. The preacher was in the pulpit by this time, and he was preaching so hard and loud he woke up the kids who were already asleep.

Then, to our amazement, something came flying out of his mouth as he was preaching at the top of his lungs and waving his hands. It was a set of false teeth, both the uppers and lowers. He jumped down out of the pulpit, grabbed his teeth, put them back in his mouth, and kept on preaching.

We kids stared, but we didn't dare laugh out loud because we knew a hickory switch would be waiting at home for us if we did. We spent the rest of the sermon nudging each other to stay awake, just in case something else happened.

Mable Ann Hemphill

Didn't I Tell Y'all?

In the early years, sharecroppers' children worked very hard in the field. If the father died or went missing, Heaven help the oldest child, especially if he was male because he worked even harder.

But by the time I was born, in the 1950's, things were a little better in some families, sometimes.

Also, you have to remember that these were before the days of Toys R Us, so sharecropper kids made their own fun.

Now, when you were over to some other child's house, any old person could whip your tail. Then she would tell your grandma, who whipped your tail then told your momma when she got home from work, and tired though she was, she whipped your tail with your own hickory switch that she'd made you go get. And you better not get a little one or else you really got a whipping. And you had to get one to her likin's, or else grandma would get one with three prongs, plait it, and whip you again.

Anyway, on this particular day the neighborhood kids and I were out playing our usual games: "Ain't no bears out tonight," "Pop Whip," or a game with my toy that PawPaw made called the Zizzy Button.

We got tired of those games after a while, and decided to go to the Katy Hole. I am not telling the story about going swimming in the wintertime, but if the people who were in that escapade are still alive when this book comes out, they might remember and get a good laugh.

Now mind you, the Katy Hole was a long way down in the woods, and it was the winter time. No kids were allowed to go down there, and very few adults ever went of their own accord. But we were hard headed and decided to sneak off. We had gone a good ways, when we heard a loud roaring sound like a freight train or a tornado. Instead of turning around and going back, we went on. We went down into the woods a bit farther, looked through trees, and there it was.

The Katy Hole was where the creek made a bend like when you bend your arm, swirling the water into an enormous whirlpool! It was the most God-awful sight we had ever seen in our lives, and we never want to see again. It was extremely loud and scary, and you did not want to fall in because you would never, ever be found.

Well, we took off running back home. When we got out of the woods, we rested and took deep breaths. Everyone knew never to tell what we saw, because if one child told, everybody's tails would get a whipping for days on end.

I decided to keep this secret for life. I never told Mommae, but sometimes, I think she'd suspect. And some of the other kids' parents knew something, because we were very good children for months afterward. Mommae would say, "Y'all actin' too good. You must a' done somethin'!"

I would say, "No ma-am," and never look up, because I couldn't tell a lie too straight.

Sometimes now, it seems as if I can hear Mommae saying, in her own Southern way, "Didn't I tell y'all?"

THE RALEIGH MAN

In the old days, one thing you could count on as sure as the turning seasons was the peddler coming by. We called him the Raleigh Man. He was always a white man. Although, if a peddler died, his wife usually took over the regular route in order to feed their family.

The woman of the house always dealt with the Raleigh Man and did the transactions, which helped so much. And if she couldn't read, there was always a kid in the family that could, when he was allowed. Most of the time they had to work the farm, and school was not an option.

The Raleigh Man had a regular route, so he knew all the people and gave the sharecroppers credit. The sharecroppers always paid on time, and never allowed their debt to grow any larger than five dollars; a whole lot in the early 1950's.

The Raleigh Man always had an assortment of flavors like vanilla, vanilla extract, lemon, and lemon extract, that were used in cakes and pies. He carried cake pans, measuring utensils, and all the other tools for baking. He always carried some type of salve and liniment with him, too.

Now, before the Raleigh Man, the sharecropper would use petroleum jelly mixed with something, and before that, lard mixed with sulfur or turpentine to rub on sores. But after the Raleigh Man arrived on the scene, there came a small change in medicine. His salve had a real medicinal smell, and sometimes a color added to it.

The one thing that became a medicinal staple to the sharecropper that the Raleigh Man carried was called Pneumonia Salve. It had a strong smell, and was thick and white and came in a small, flat can about one inch high. It was used for colds in the winter. They would put it on your chest, put some around your nose, put you to bed, and let you sweat the cold out.

The yellow salve would be used on old people for aches and pains. It looked like it would burn paint off a can. The liniments were worse, and you really didn't want to get hold of any of them; ask my brother, Mike.

These salves were used in poultices to get rid of boils if you did not want to use hog meat, or "fat back" as we called it. The plain one with a nice smell, along with sulfur, would heal sores on kids' bodies or tetter in kids' scalps. Most of the time, tetter, or ring worm, was killed with black walnut leaves that were rolled, chopped up, and rubbed in the kid's hair. But the salve worked faster.

As time wore on, things began to change, and the Raleigh Man was no longer an integral part of life in the South.

Mable Ann Hemphill

Letters to My Teachers from the Sharecropper's Desk

Eighth Grade Classroom
Roosevelt School

Dear Mr. Wilbur Lewis Brown,

Thank you for teaching me the importance of having a good character.

You were always a snappy dresser, with a neat haircut and shiny shoes. Even though all the teachers in those years came to school well dressed, you stood out.

You always took pride in character. You made sure that I reached for the top rung in life, even though it seemed an impossible thing to do at the time.

I was an A student. Everyone in your class had to have their homework done as neatly as possible, and turned in on time.

But a change was coming. You could feel it in the air. I remember you and another teacher coming to our small, three room shanty to talk to my real father, not PawPaw. You talked with Mommae also.

Then the change was here; it was time for integration, and not everyone was happy. Someone had to be a pioneer, and I was one of the kids chosen to go. Looking back, the only thing I remember from those months of preparation was sneaking barbecue potato chips into your class when I wasn't supposed to. You made me write the brand name of the chips on the blackboard, and "um good." I never ate in class again, no matter how hungry I was.

I had no idea how important this new step was for all of us. After class, you put it in words I could understand.

"Miss Mable Ann," you said. "Things are going to change for you, and others. But someone has to go and help make a bigger change possible. Everyone cannot go right now, but you can. You can go and make a difference."

Mr. Brown, you and the other teachers from Roosevelt School in Clover, South Carolina, had done your best to equip us to be the pioneers of integration in the rural South during the 1960's. You taught us to do our best in spite of our new surroundings, and not to lose our character.

So, for all that you and others did for us, I most humbly thank you.

    Sincerely,
    Miss Mable Ann

Let the Lord Do His Work

Any African American who grew up in a sharecropping family can remember tell a version of this story.

It was hot as two hells in rural South Carolina that day but, the weather man had predicted a storm brewing, so all of the people in the field finished their work and came inside. Even though we had our own house, we so happened to be at my cousins' house with a lot of other kids on this day.

One thing about the elders who lived during that time in the rural South was their respect for each other. They always looked out for one another, and though they loved God, they had their own customs for how to behave during a thunderstorm.

We looked up at the sky, and everything seemed to suddenly grow dark. The storm finally got up. It was raining buckets outside, and everyone inside was sitting still, either in chairs if they were adults, or on the wood floor if they were kids. All of a sudden, my cousin decided he wanted to get up and get something.

Immediately, I heard a whack, and everyone knew what it was. It was not the sound of lightning, or the storm, but the wound of one of the adults whacking him upside the head.

The woman who'd smacked him spoke real soft in his ear, "Didn't I tell you to sit down and let the Lord do his work?"

Everyone else, including him, knew better than to get up during a thunderstorm. We all knew to sit down around the wall, like little chickens in a huddle, so the Lord could "do his work." And now, when I witness thunderstorms, I still will sometimes hear the words of my ancestors saying, "Sit down and let the Lord do his work."

Angel with the Strange Arms

It was hot as a firecracker that day, and we were still living on the Ridge Road in Clover. So PawPaw decided to go over to our Aunt Neely and Uncle John's house in Gastonia, North Carolina. I have no idea where Mike and Andy were, but anyway, we "took out to going," as they say in the South.

We had gone up the road toward Gastonia, and we turned off on a dirt road where we had to cross a rickety old bridge. As we went up the hill in PawPaw's 1951 Ford, PawPaw got sick. I was scared, but he reassured me that everything was going to be fine as soon as we got to my uncle and aunt's house. But things took a turn for the worse when we had to take a sharp corner, and slid over into a deep ditch on the side of the road.

Now mind you, this was before cell phones, and there were very few house phones for that matter. And us being colored folk, we wouldn't have been allowed to use a public phone if there had been any nearby.

PawPaw put his foot to the gas and tried and tried, but that car was not coming out of the ditch. Then, to make matters worse, PawPaw had an asthma attack. He started praying, and I bowed my head and joined in because we were taught to bow in the presence of the Lord. Then PawPaw asked God to send an angel to our rescue. I kept looking for somebody with some wings to show up and get us out of the ditch.

Well, the angel was a white man on a tractor and he didn't have wings. He did have strange arms, though. They stood out stiff from his body, not bending as he gripped the tractor's steering wheel, and they looked pasty against the rest of his tanned skin.

He had seen us go into the ditch, and he knew PawPaw because he said, "John Andy, I've come to get you out of this ditch. I can pull you out, and I ain't gonna charge you nothing cause y'all good people."

So he proceeded to pull us out of the ditch and away we went, but we turned around and went back home because PawPaw wasn't feeling good.

I thank God for that nice white man who came to our rescue. I never knew who he was, and now I realize he was an amputee. If by some chance this book gets to his descendants, I'd like to thank him, on behalf of my grandfather and me, with all of our hearts.

SODA WATER

The air was crisp and the wind was brisk. PawPaw wasn't feeling well, and he was wheezing something fierce. So he decided to lie down in the front room on the couch near the wood heater and rest a bit. Mommae had told me and Mike and Andy to get ready for bed because we had to go to school the next day. We had plenty of kindling to make a good fire so the house was toasty warm and since we only had three rooms and we all slept in one bedroom in three beds.

PawPaw was lying with his face toward the inside of the couch and he was getting more and more restless.

Around 12 o'clock I heard PawPaw call out my name. "Mable Ann, get me some soda water. Back then a lot of the old sharecroppers used homemade remedies for their ailments and baking soda and water was a staple. PawPaw had what sharecropping folk called a "chicken breast". He was a WW1 veteran who came home with major health problems including heart trouble and asthma. He would have asthma attacks so bad that he would have to go outside and sit on the front porch just so he could breathe. So even though it was cold outside that is just what he did. I got him his wooden straight chair so that he could sit upright. He was still breathing and wheezing heavily.

I heard Mommae say, "John Andy, you need Dr. Perry." Now mind you this was in the days of segregation but Dr. Perry was one in a million, so he made sure all of his patients were cared for. So even though blacks and whites had separate visitation rooms, (coloreds entered through the back everywhere), he was a very caring doctor.

By this time it was about one o'clock in the morning and PawPaw was getting sicker and weaker. Just then Doctor Perry showed up with his black doctor's bag. "Get John Andy in the house" is what Dr. Perry said. And that is what we did. Dr.Perry began checking PawPaw's chest and his blood pressure.

After Dr. Perry got PawPaw to feeling better with some small pills that he had in his bag, he left but said for PawPaw to come to the office as soon as he got up. So we all went to bed and PawPaw laid down on the couch again.

It was around 7am in the morning and we were all up "stirrin' around" meaning we were getting prepared for the day in sharecropper's language). "Mableann, get me some soda water 'for you go to school" is what PawPaw asked me to do. "Yes sir" I said, and I got a glass from the pantry in the kitchen of our three room home and put a teaspoon of baking soda and some water from the tin bucket with a homemade dipper made out of a dried gourd from the garden. I don't know why I got a glass because most sharecropping families often drank from a can because it kept whatever you were drinking colder, especially tea. But this morning I reached up and got a glass. He drank it and said "thank you, baby girl" and sat the glass on the floor and laid back down on the couch with his face turned toward the inside of the couch. Mommae was in the kitchen and me and my brothers were in the bedroom getting ready for school. I walked out to check on my beloved PawPaw when I saw him turn over real fast and fall off of the couch. He hit his head on the glass when he fell and had a cut and it was bleeding. Mommae was screaming as were my brothers Mike and Andy. We tried to pick him up and couldn't. Being the oldest and although I was only twelve years old and raised by sharecroppers, I had to go into action because that is what the oldest children were raised up to do, so I didn't have time to cry, so I ran outside and looked around and there was no one to be seen. We had done all that we could do so I just simply said, "God, please help us!!!!" About that time I looked and there was a "colored" man (back then we were called, "colored") walking near our mailbox, so I screamed "please come help us, my PawPaw has fallen off the couch and we can't get him up". The unknown man never said anything but just walked with me into the house, scooped up PawPaw, put him back on the couch and walked back out of the door and never said a word to anyone. We would have never got PawPaw up if it had not been for this unknown person. PawPaw's eyes and mouth were shut and his arms were already folded. I ran back outside to say thank you to the unknown man but it seemed that he had vanished. PawPaw was gone. He had suffered a heart attack. Daddy was working in the cotton mill so he came home as soon as he could.

Both Dr. Perry and the undertaker came really soon. Dr. Perry pronounced him dead and the undertaker came and took him away while my brothers and I were crying and Mommae was wailing and walking behind the gurney as they put PawPaw in the hearse. I remember standing on the front porch knowing that our life was really changing again now. What would we do?

Mommae and I sat down to get Pawpaw's obituary done. My daddy and brothers picked out clothes. The next few days were very sad but we all pulled through. We all sat on the front row of Liberty Hill AME Zion Church near PawPaw's flag draped casket. People of the church all came around and shook our hands. Afterward the hymn choir began to sing one of those old Negro spirituals.

This was 1962 and a southern church in the country with a wood floor and most of the church folk were sharecroppers, so the people made their own music by patting their feet. Years earlier in some rural black churches they used wash boards or tin cases. (The Fire-Baptized churches always had tambourines.) They sang and sang. PawPaw was one of the leaders and the founding fathers of Liberty Hill AME Zion Church in Clover SC, so his name was placed on the Cornerstone of the church which was a place of honor and part of history. I always feel so blessed when I get a chance to visit our home church. Thank you so much PawPaw!! I miss you still.

MEDICINAL PURPOSES

Sharecroppers never thought about going to the doctor much during the early years. And most of the older people had their own remedies which had been handed down through the generations. I remember one day when I was over at my great aunt's house and got my little finger slammed in the wooden door on the back of the house.

That finger was bleeding real badly. It seemed that there was blood everywhere! There was a nice size gash in it too!! Well, my great aunt said, "Gal, bring that finger here to me." She poured some water from the well into a tin wash pan and got some homemade lye soap (she never used store bought soap, it cost too much and she didn't believe in it anyway) and washed my finger off while I sobbed. Then she took the lamp shade and the globe off the kerosene lamp, stuck my finger in the kerosene, got some soot from the chimney, wrapped my finger up with a clean rag and said, "Go back out in the yard and play. You'll be alright! Grown folk be talkin." When I heard those words I took myself and my sore kerosene smellin', sooty finger and went back outside and played.

Every sharecropper farming community always had a midwife to help with birthing the babies. In the early years before birth certificates for "negroes or colored folk", when a baby was born the midwife would record the baby's birth in the family Bible or record it somewhere so it wouldn't get lost. This was most definitely after slavery because in previous years we were known as property so we were logged in the books sometimes along with the livestock.

I cannot even imagine having to boil water and assist midwives in birthin' babies.

Most sharecropping communities had a medicine person who could cure stuff or they themselves knew how to "make medicine".

Every spring the children of sharecroppers knew what was coming. "Spring Tonic!!!". Everybody hated hearing that name. Every spring the children in the family would get lined up and given a concoction to clean you out, and clean you out it would!! Now remember this was in the time of no inside bathrooms and the soft toilet tissue was not even on this earth yet (or poor folk didn't have any) so toilet tissue that scratched your behind or old newspapers was the norm.

When the men were working in the fields they would just go into the woods and use leaves.

I hated taking this spring tonic. Some of the old time southern, country stores still carried some of the liquids used along with sap from the pine tree and sulfur to clean you out right up throughout the 1960's. Old people said it took the "Yuma" out of your blood. If that meant giving you the runs, well it did its job. One thing it did was kill any parasite that you had in your body.

They also used black walnut leaves. They would collect them and crush them and use them to kill ring worm and tetter on their kid's body. One kid I remember had worms so bad that he had dark circles round his eyes. So his grandma rubbed some kerosene on his forehead, gave him some tonic mixed with a something that would be toxic now and he got better. Some older people used a flower called foxglove. We now know that it is good for heart problems.

The old men (including my daddy and all of his friends) made a tonic of yellow root and white liquor from the still. He said it was good for them. 'Said it gave them courage. I never knew what it meant back then or why he said it gave the men "courage". After thinking about it now, it sounds like an earlier form of "that little blue pill".

Shame on you, Daddy!!! Shame on you!!!

In the fall while the kids were gathering pine for the kindling because the winters seemed like they were real cold back then, the older members of the family would go into the woods and gather leaves from this plant that looked like a fuzzy flower to make cold medicine.

If you had a sore throat you gargled with warm salt water and then you got chopped up onion tied up in a clean white rag tied around your throat to take out the soreness.

There was also a healer in the community who would be a woman. I remember getting burned real bad on the underside of my wrist. It had a great big blister on it. I don't know how she knew but along came Aunt Plume. Well I was screaming something awful!! She said, "Gal, gimme yo' hand!" And she jerked my hand and held it and began what sharecroppers call "talkin' the fire out." I couldn't understand what she was saying but the blister went down and my hand quit hurting. Then the old people put some kind of homemade salve made from lard and some herbs from the yard on it and wrapped it up with a clean rag. Then sent me out in the yard with the rest of the kids. To this day, I never had a scar.

When a mother had her baby, she would always take her baby as soon as she could to the "healer lady". Folks in the rural south said she had "healing power". The healer would blow in the baby's mouth so the baby wouldn't get "thrash" "known as thrush, in its mouth. She even knew when the young women would be "in a family way" sometimes before they even knew. She would say," Gal, you gon' have a youngun. I can tell by the way you walk. Look's like it's gonna be a (boy or girl) child". And then she would proceed to tell them what it was and she hit it on the money every time. She told me, "Mable Ann, somethings peculiar 'bout. You know you born with a vail over your face. God say he gon' use you." I never knew what she meant so I said "Thank you mam"and I would often go talk with her and she would tell me things about her "growins' up" as she called it.

I learned so much about my ancestors and history itself from this wonderful lady. She was real wrinkly, I thought back then, because she was so old, but she was so very smart and very wise. She would always tell me, "Gal, God say he gon' use you keep doin' what you do and one day yo' wisdom gon' kick in and he gon' do just what he said." I am still waiting for that day to come.

Letters to My Teachers from the Sharecropper's Desk

Biology Classroom
Clover High School

Dear Mrs. Barbara Norman,

Thank you for your extremely caring ways.

Integration was a new step for me and others. I remember feeling like a square peg in a round hole, it seemed as though I just didn't fit. But you were my angel. You had heard of the bad things happening in the school to us colored students that first year. No one knew what to do, or what to say, or what was correct, most times.

But you made a decision to take a skinny black girl under your wing, and no one knew it or even realized it.

Once a week, you would take me home with you to iron your family's clothes. Or at least, that is what I thought, and so did other people. I needed the money, so I was glad to get a job.

But that was not what you had planned, because I really was not at ironing. You took that time to show me what it felt like to be loved and appreciated for myself, and not for the color of my skin. You and your family were so nice.

You taught me to pay attention to detail. You even helped me with my studies at your house. You talked to me in a way that you couldn't talk to me at school, because you would have been ridiculed.

You affectionately called me "Little Miss Mable Ann," and worked with me as I struggled through hard assignments. You always told me to do my best, and to treat others the way I wanted to be treated. Your family and kids were so nice to me at your home.

Then, you began to teach me to overcome my difficulties. You would say, "You can and will make it, and often times the easiest way is not the best way."

When I would mess up ironing, you and I would do it over, together. No one even knew, and I could only tell people what a good teacher you were at school. I really wanted to say how good you were to me in your home, and how you made me feel that I could accomplish anything.

I remember the day you told me, "Little Miss Mable Ann, dream and dream big. Always dream big! You will accomplish your dreams."

For taking time out for me, I most humbly thank you.

Sincerely,
Miss Mable Ann

Mable Ann Hemphill

A Negro Killing in a Southern Town

It was, as I recall, a winter morning in 1962. I remember the year because PawPaw was real sick at the time, and he died on December 10th, 1962. I cannot remember what day in the week it was when this all happened, but it began with a knock at the door. It was the lady who taught us kids Bible School during the summer, she lived on Ridge Road. She had been to our small house before, and we had been to hers for a visit or two. She was married, but her husband was not with her. This was not her ordinary knock. This time her knock was different, and it came early in the morning.

We opened the door, and she came in and sat down. She looked frantic. The older people always made the kids go somewhere else while they talked "grown folk business," as they called it. Then some other people came to house who had been coming regularly for a while. I cannot remember them by name, but I do remember this lady.

Apparently, there had been a killing in Gastonia, North Carolina, a few days before. Gastonia was a neighboring town of Clover, South Carolina. There had been a killing of a young Negro man by a white doctor at the home of someone in the young man's family. I heard them say, "He stuck that butcher knife in that young man's stomach and cut him. There won't be nothin' done about it."

This lady and my grandmother sat over in the corner on one side of the wood stove, and my grandfather and two other men sat on the other. They were all gathered around the wood stove in our front room to keep warm. PawPaw got out a piece of paper and wrote something down. He was in charge of the meeting because he could read and write.

These people sitting in our front room had been coming to our house before, but mostly in the evening and never together. If they did go to each other's houses during the week, they would sing songs and have prayer meetings.

Now, even though they came to our house at different times, I learned that there was a movement of the NAACP coming into the area, and it was being organized at our house, with my grandfather taking a lead role. It was a movement that would not have been accepted by the Southern white people nearby at this time.

So everything was done ever so quietly.

But this killing of a young Negro man in Gastonia gave colored folk, with my sickly Army Veteran Sharecropper grandfather at the helm, a vibrant vigor to forge ahead.

Thank God for PawPaw and others who used our small, three room house t organize our local branch of the NAACP, and to be pioneers for the Advancement of People of Color in rural South Carolina.

His Plan

Now we come to that momentous day in January, 2009.

With an eighty dollar ticket in my pocket, I set out with my friends from work on an all day bus trip.

It was cold, and we had traveled, like everyone else, from far and near to witness this day. But what was happening still had not hit us. Then someone on the bus said, "Folks, we are in Washington D.C." A quiet stillness came over the passengers, and I looked out and saw a monument of some kind. Then what we were going to witness took over in my mind.

We were about to witness history. I started to cry, but I didn't want anyone to see me. I got my coat and began to pin the old pictures and my grandparents' Marriage Certificate from 1937 to the inside lining.

Finally, we arrived. Since I am from the South, even though the sun was shining, the Washington climate was deathly cold to me.

When we got off the bus, my friends all turned left, but I accidentally turned right. I had somehow gotten away from my group and found myself walking in a great press of people all going one way. I couldn't turn around and go back. There were thousands in this river of people, so I had to go with the flow.

I briefly looked down and saw a small rock. Very quickly, I picked it up, put it in my pocket, and kept on walking. Finally, I found myself at the Washington Monument alongside thousands of others.

And everyone had a story. Some about how their forefathers came to this country with nothing, worked hard, and made a good living for their future family. I didn't have a story. I was there by chance on an eighty dollar bus trip with a story that wasn't mine. It was my grandparents', and I was simply there to tell it for them.

And tell it I did! I told their story to people who were there not only from America, but from other parts of the world. I opened my coat, and people from all over the world started snapping pictures. Pictures of my ancestors! They would have been so proud to be alive and witnessing history being made. The people who were snapping pictures had gotten so close to me that I was leaning on the protective wiring around the monument. I was freezing, but I was showing their pictures that I had saved.

Everyone was happy, hugging each other, smiling and talking, all bundled up with coats and hats and gloves.

Suddenly, I heard a still, small voice saying, "Look at the faces."

I began to look not only at the faces, but to hear the sounds of happiness. I then began to realize that there was no awareness of race, creed, color, national origins, religious beliefs, sexual preferences, or gender there that day at the Washington Monument. There was no "I am richer" than you are." There was no "I am Native American." There was no" I am African American," or whatever American you were because "it" was not there. There was only brotherly or sisterly love for our fellow man or woman.

It was as though the earth had taken in a breath of fresh air. And for that moment in time, as we all stood very proudly there at the Washington Monument, there was no Hate. It was not there! It did not exist or have a place there.

There at the Washington Monument, on that day, for that moment in time as we witnessed history, we were all very proud Americans.

Then Aretha Franklin began to sing, "My country 'tis of thee, sweet land of liberty…" and it really hit! I looked over, and you could see tears on the cheeks of individuals there. It was as though the weight of hundreds of years of racism and hatred had, at this moment in time, been lifted from the shoulders of these people. These Americans. I looked, and some Americans were holding on to each other. Others had their hands on their hearts as I did.

So, as Aretha sang "My Country 'Tis of Thee," I felt so proud to be an American. Racism and hatred did not exist. It had been replaced with love for America and our fellow man.

I felt so proud to be the great-great-granddaughter of a slave known only as Prince, to be the great-granddaughter and the granddaughter of sharecroppers and maids who worked to make this country great, to come from being a colored girl in rural South Carolina, to being not only African American, but an American.

So I reached in the right pocket of my coat and got my small rock, the pebble. I got it out, held it up, and briefly closed my eyes. I said to my beloved ancestors who had gone on before, especially PawPaw and Mommae, "This one is for you."

Mable Ann Bigger-Hemphill, March 30th, 2014.

About The Author

Born Mable Ann Bigger on November 12, 1951, to then George and Deloris Bigger (now Mrs. Warren Stewart). She was raised by her grandparents John Andy and Mary Gwinn Bigger, a sickly Army Veteran sharecropper and his wife, an illiterate maid in rural Clover, South Carolina.

Mable was taught to read and write by the age of two

by her grandfather. Having these skills, she blossomed and enjoyed her grandfather's favorite book, the Bible.

Her talent for writing was noticed as a small child in the third grade at Roosevelt School, a segregated elementary school in Clover, South Carolina, by her teacher named Mrs. Matrue Smith. Mable wrote her first poem entitled "May Is Fifth In Line". Her poem was published in the "Evening Herald" now "The Herald" in Rock Hill, South Carolina.

This dynamic woman was a pioneer of integration in the 1960's. She was one of a group of students who were selected to begin attending Clover High School, a then, all white school, in Clover South Carolina.

Mable went on to graduate from Clover High School in Clover South Carolina. She then attended Central Piedmont College in Charlotte, North Carolina.

"Miss Mable", as she is affectionately called, has a true love for people. She is the epitome of the "true missionary". She began this journey as a small child when she started working in the church alongside the older ladies. Her passion is to give whatever assistance needed to help individuals overcome their meager surrounding and thereby aid them to "getting out of the revolving door" of poverty. Her heart is filled with compassion for "THE LEAST, THE LOST AND THE LEFT OUT". She has been awarded numerous for accolades for her work throughout her 20+years of volunteerism.

Her volunteer efforts have been noted by the following institutions:

- NAACP AWARD for her work on homelessness and race relations

- ECKERD DRUG STORES SALUTE TO 100 WOMEN for her work on homelessness and women's issues

- CITY OF GASTONIA North Carolina for her work in volunteerism to combat homelessness

- GASTON COUNTY for her work in volunteerism to combat homelessness and women's issues

- CHAMBER OF COMMERCE CITY OF GASTONIA AND GASTON COUNTY as BUSINESS ADVOCATE OF THE YEAR for her work in starting the Minority Business Development Corp which assisted all women and minorities in starting their own small business

- 1994 - Entrepreneur of the Year Award

- Selected to work on the Whitehouse Conference on Small Business under President Bill Clinton

Mable has two grown children Jarvis and Cherrish and she makes her home in Charlotte, North Carolina.

Mable has a saying, "Stay focused, through strong belief in your higher power, belief in yourself and a strong determination, it will come to pass." She often says, "I am the could have been, the should have been, the would have been, if it had not been for the gracious favor of an Almighty God."

www.ingramcontent.com/pod-product-compliance
Lightning Source LLC
Chambersburg PA
CBHW071226160426
43196CB00012B/2429